HOW
FAST
IS A
CHEETAH?

Illustrated by
Tudor Humphries

Written by
Jinny Johnson

Rand McNally for Kids

Books•Maps•Atlases

A Marshall Edition
Conceived, edited, and designed by
Marshall Editions, 170 Piccadilly, London W1V 9DD

Published in the United States of America by Rand McNally & Co., 1995

Library of Congress Cataloging-in-Publication Data
Johnson, Jinny.
      How fast is a cheetah? / written by Jinny Johnson ; illustrated by
Tudor Humphries.
          p. cm.
      ISBN 0-528-83730-3
      1. Animals—Miscellanea—Juvenile literature.   2. Animal
locomotion—Miscellanea—Juvenile literature.   3. Speed–
–Miscellanea—Juvenile literature. [1. Animal locomotion.
2. Animals—Miscellanea. 3. Speed—Miscellanea.] I. Humphries,
Tudor, ill. II. Title.
QL49.J62   1995
501. 1'852—dc20   94-47266
                                          CIP
                                          AC

Managing Editor: Kate Phelps
Designer: Ian Winton
Art Director: Branka Surla
Editorial Director: Cynthia O'Brien

Printed and bound in Italy
by Officine Grafiche De
Agostini – Novara

Contents

How fast can a racehorse run?

The best racehorses can run at more than 40 miles an hour—faster than most cars go in a city. The fastest a racehorse has ever run is just over 43 miles an hour. This was in a short race of a quarter of a mile. Most racehorses belong to a breed of horses called thoroughbreds. They are slender but strong, with long, slim legs.

Olympic athletes run at more than 22 miles an hour for short distances. They cover a distance of 110 yards—about the length of a football field—in under 10 seconds.

Greyhounds are much faster than human sprinters. The quickest speed for racing greyhounds is more than 40 miles an hour.

All of these runners are sprinters. This means they can only keep up these speeds over short distances.

Did you know that a jack rabbit can run faster than a racehorse?

A jack rabbit can run at up to 45 miles an hour. Speed helps it to escape from enemies such as foxes.

How fast is a cheetah?

Cheetahs run faster than any other animal.
They can race along at up to 65 miles an hour—
faster than a car traveling on the freeway. Can you
see the car hidden in the grass?

The cheetah is a sprinter. It cannot keep running
at this pace for more than a minute or so.

Did you know that a cheetah can go as fast as a car?

The cheetah runs fast to catch
animals to eat, such as
gazelles, rabbits, and even
young ostriches. It gets as
near to the prey as possible,
then chases after it as fast as
it can go.

The pronghorn antelope is not quite as fast as the cheetah—but it keeps going longer. A pronghorn can run at 40 miles an hour for 10 minutes. Even a young pronghorn can outrun a horse.

Pronghorns live in North America and cheetahs live in Africa, so the two would never meet in the wild.

A pronghorn runs to escape from enemies such as mountain lions and wolves.

How slow is a sloth?

The sloth is one of the slowest of all land animals. It lives in the South American jungle where it hangs upside down from a branch of a tree. From time to time, it pulls itself along the branch to look for leaves to eat.

The giant tortoise takes about a minute to move only 20 feet. A child could walk that distance in a few seconds. Can you see the children hidden here?

Once a week the sloth climbs down to the ground where it travels even more slowly than it does in the trees. It drags itself along at about six feet a minute.

Did you know that a sloth moves along branches at only 15 feet a minute?

The garden snail is even slower than the sloth and the giant tortoise. It takes about an hour to go 50 or 60 feet. That is about twice the width of a tennis court.

How far can a kangaroo jump?

Kangaroos are champion jumpers. They travel at up to 40 miles an hour by leaping along on their strong back legs. Kangaroos live in Australia, and many of them spend most of their time in the desert. They may need to travel 20 miles for a drink of water so moving quickly is important.

The springbok is a kind of gazelle and it is a good jumper, too. If frightened by a lion or other enemy, it leaps high into the air.

The longest a red kangaroo has ever jumped is 42 feet in one bound. This is as long as nine children lying down. Can you find the children hidden in the sand?

Did you know that a kangaroo can jump more than 40 feet?

A gray kangaroo has leapt eight feet—as high as two seven-year-old children standing on each other's shoulders. Can you see the children hidden in the bush?

A springbok can leap seven or eight feet into the air. This leaping is known as pronking or stotting and warns other members of the herd that danger is near.

13

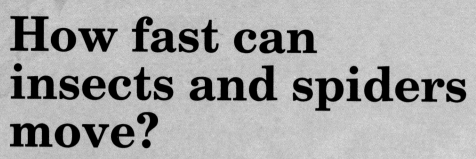

How fast can insects and spiders move?

Although insects are small they can travel at surprisingly fast speeds. Cockroaches are among the quickest. They have wings but do not use them often. Instead, they scurry along on their long legs.

Some kinds of cockroaches can move at about three miles an hour.

Fast-moving sunspiders are related to spiders and scorpions. They are sometimes called windscorpions because they run like the wind. Sunspiders live in hot, dry places. They catch insects and other small creatures to eat.

Cockroaches stay hidden during the day. At night, they come out to look for food. They eat almost anything—even paper.

Speedy sunspiders run at up to 10 miles an hour—probably faster than you can rollerskate.

Did you know that a sunspider can run faster than you?

How far can insects jump?

One champion jumper in the insect world is the click beetle. It can jump as high as 12 inches—more than 25 times its own length. The click beetle jumps to escape from its enemies.

The click beetle is less than half an inch long, but it springs into the air with greater force for its size than a space rocket taking off from the earth.

The clicking sound it makes as it leaps into the air gives the click beetle its name.

The tiny flea is another record breaker. It can leap more than 150 times its own length. If a human being could do this, he or she would be able to jump from the ground to the top of a skyscraper.

A flea lives in the fur of an animal such as a cat. Fleas are only a fraction of an inch long. Here a flea is seen through a magnifying glass.

Did you know that a flea can leap up to eight inches?

How fast can a snake wriggle?

Even though snakes don't have legs, they move surprisingly quickly. The black mamba, which lives in Africa, travels along the ground or a tree branch at six or seven miles an hour. But it can move as fast as 12 miles an hour for short bursts.

Did you know that the black mamba is the fastest of all snakes?

The sidewinder snake moves more slowly than the mamba at about four miles an hour. It travels along with a strange sideways motion, leaving a row of marks in the sand.

The fastest-moving lizard is the six-lined racerunner. This long, slim lizard can run at up to 18 miles an hour, much quicker than the fastest snake. It runs to catch prey such as insects, spiders, and scorpions to eat.

The racerunner lizard and the black mamba can move nearly as fast as a pet cat. Can you find a cat hidden in the sand?

A black mamba measures up to 13 feet long—more than twice as long as an adult human. It eats birds, lizards, mice, and other small creatures which it kills with its poisonous fangs.

The racerunner lizard's speed is useful when it is in danger. It makes a swift dash to the safety of a rock or burrow.

Which is the fastest sea creature?

Water is many times thicker than air, so sea creatures have to work much harder than land animals to move fast. They have to push themselves through the water with flippers and fins. It is difficult to measure how quickly sea creatures move, but people think the sailfish is the fastest swimmer.

The gentoo penguin is the fastest swimming bird. It can move at up to 17 miles an hour for short distances.

The leatherback is the biggest and the fastest moving of all sea turtles. Its top speed is about 22 miles an hour.

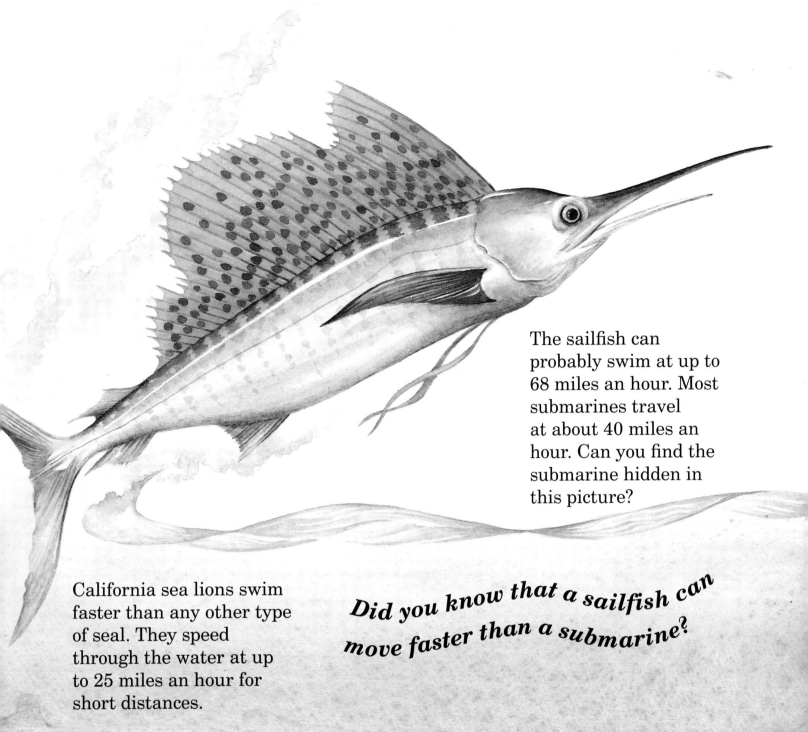

The sailfish can probably swim at up to 68 miles an hour. Most submarines travel at about 40 miles an hour. Can you find the submarine hidden in this picture?

California sea lions swim faster than any other type of seal. They speed through the water at up to 25 miles an hour for short distances.

Did you know that a sailfish can move faster than a submarine?

Which is the fastest whale?

All whales and dolphins have streamlined, torpedo-shaped bodies—an ideal shape for moving quickly in water. The fastest is probably the killer whale, which can swim at a speed of 35 miles an hour for a short time. When not hunting, the whale cruises along at about 10 miles an hour.

A whale is not a fish but a mammal like a dog or human. A fish swims by moving its tail from side to side. A whale swims by moving its tail up and down.

The squid swims in a different way from most other sea creatures. It shoots jets of water out of its body to propel itself along at up to 20 miles an hour.

Killer whales are among the fiercest hunters in the sea. They eat fish, squid, seals, and penguins and need to be able to move fast to catch them. Killer whales live and hunt in family groups called pods. A full-grown killer whale measures up to 30 feet—longer than two cars.

Did you know that a whale can move as fast as a windsurfer?

In this picture you are looking up at the whale from underneath. Can you see the windsurfer riding on top of the water?

How fast can birds fly?

Some of the fastest flying birds are ducks and geese such as the common eider, the spur-winged goose, and the red-breasted merganser. All these birds fly at more than 40 miles an hour and may even reach speeds of as much as 65 miles an hour.

Racing pigeons are speedy birds, too. They can fly at 45 to 50 miles an hour.

Common eider

Spur-winged goose

The swiftest bird of all is the peregrine falcon. It catches other birds to eat and makes astonishingly fast dives through the air to seize its prey with its hooked claws. Some dives have been timed at more than 112 miles an hour. When flying normally, the falcon travels at up to 60 miles an hour.

Did you know that a peregrine falcon can dive through the air at more than 100 miles an hour?

Red-breasted merganser

Many geese and ducks are strong, fast fliers. They make regular journeys over hundreds of miles between winter and summer homes.

At top speed, a peregrine falcon can fly as fast as a small airplane. Can you find the airplane hidden here?

25

How fast can a bird run?

The ostrich is too big to fly but it is a high-speed runner. It travels at speeds of at least 45 miles an hour and perhaps as much as 60 miles an hour. Its long legs and large strong feet help the ostrich to run fast.

Chickens rarely fly but are not very fast runners. They scuttle around at speeds of only a few miles an hour.

The greater roadrunner can fly but generally runs instead. It moves at about 12 miles an hour—faster than most people can run.

It is important for the ostrich to be able to move quickly because it often has to run to escape enemies such as lions. Also, it lives in dry lands in southern Africa and needs to travel long distances to find plants to eat.

Running at top speed an ostrich could keep ahead of a racing cyclist.

Did you know that an ostrich can run faster than any other bird?

Which animal wins the race?

In a race of all the record breakers in this book, the cheetah would win on land, the sailfish in the sea, and the peregrine falcon in the air. Humans would be left behind!

Who would have
thought that an ostrich
could run as fast as a
racehorse? Look at the
animals running on
land and see what other
surprises you can find.

Birds have no rivals in
the air. And the swiftest
birds can fly as fast as a
small airplane.

A human swimmer would
be far behind most of
these sea creatures. Even
a champion can only
manage about five or
six miles an hour for
short distances.

Index